The Essential Guide to Graphic Design Success

Disclaimer

This book is designed to provide information on how to achieve success in the graphic design trade. This information is provided and sold with the knowledge that the publisher and author do not offer any legal or other professional advice. In the case of a need for any such expertise consult with the appropriate professional. This book does not contain all information available on the subject. This book has not been created to be specific to any individual's or organizations' situation or needs. Every effort has been made to make this book as accurate as possible. However, there may be typographical and or content errors. Therefore, this book should serve only as a general guide and not as the ultimate source of subject information. This book contains information that might be dated and is intended only to educate and entertain. The author and publisher shall have no liability or responsibility to any person or entity regarding any loss or damage incurred, or alleged to have been incurred, directly or indirectly, by the information contained in this book. You hereby agree to be bound by this disclaimer or you may return this book within the guarantee time period for a full refund.

Table of Contents

Introduction

Nowadays, we cannot escape the need for graphic design – graphics surround us. Walk past the park, and you will see a sign that keeps people off the grass. Ride a train, and an infographic on how to get a ticket will guide you. Eat at a restaurant, and the layout of a menu will keep your eyes glued to the food options. All of these are graphic designs. This shows how we have become receptive to visuals and how such designs have helped us in our daily routines. It also shows the urgent need for graphic designers.

Now, the world we live in is flooded with designs. We swim through these visuals and see their various styles and functions. While doing so, we also learn to discern which designs are helpful and which are obstructive. As graphic designers, we learn techniques for constructing designs that help convey clear messages through lines, colors, and visuals. That is what this book is all about.

Graphic designers are needed, but the world does not need just another graphic designer. A lot of people have switched jobs to become graphic designers, and this career will continue to attract other professionals. Thus, to stand out within a population of designers, what we need is a knowledgeable approach filled with purpose and discipline. The world needs a graphic designer who knows how to create helpful designs. A graphic designer should know about the current trends yet still be curious enough to play with the old trends. A good designer knows that design is about more than looks and that it has the ability to influence people, consciously or subconsciously. The world needs designers like you who have the curiosity to deliver a message in a visually pleasant medium.

As you pick up this book and read through its contents, you have to understand that the visual aspect of design is still best learned with practice. The world is still a playground where graphic designers should play; this book will serve as a brief addendum to an already expansive resource about graphic design. It will break down some misconceptions about the field, develop your fundamental knowledge of visual language, and boost your confidence. This book will help you focus on skills that will help your career in graphic design.

This book – and a lot of practice – will help you learn how to become a successful graphic designer.

Chapter One: What Graphic Design Is

Type 'Golden Arches' in Google, and you'll remember a particular restaurant serving hamburgers. When you walk down the street and see a green circular logo with what looks like a mermaid within it, you'll know that place serves coffee. Even without hearing the businesses' names, you have a fair idea what they are. Their logos have been imprinted so deeply within our culture that a slight reference to one of these logos will be recognized by many people. Does this qualify those logos as great designs, though?

A lot of misconceptions surround the industry of graphic design. Some think graphic design is the same as art, in which designers are able to play with fine aesthetics for the sake of art. These people think that it doesn't matter what an image means, only that it looks like something. Others think graphic design is a skill people are born with. They think that only those who were born creative can venture into the field of graphic design. Some people are intimidated by graphic design while others merge graphic design with art. However, there's a huge difference between art and design.

Design is visual problem-solving. Design is an idea made visual. Design can look like an elaborate Rembrandt-style color painting or it can look like a preschooler's first drawing. The factors that make or break a design are the questions of how it solves a problem, how it answers questions, and how it communicates its message. The difference between art and design is that design serves a client, solves a problem, follows an objective, and presents an idea to be digested by the public – non-artists, artists and everyone in between. Designing for oneself is a myth, and a design that has no purpose or that is misunderstood is the very definition of a bad design. Design should work toward building an identity to which people can relate.

To understand the fundamentals of design, we must understand that design is effective when it's not obstructive, but at the same time, it should be visually appealing. It is able to intrigue people using visual cues without destroying its message. The problem with some designs is that they are more beautiful than effective. These poor designs focus on technique and aesthetics without considering their effect on the message. A good designer has a strong grasp on various techniques, but the best designers' works are used thoroughly by clients. Understanding the motives behind graphic design should realign our focus in our learning. We learn design techniques for a purpose – not just for beauty. With so many design techniques available for use, a designer should focus on the communicating aspect of design to reduce the clutter in his or her head.

Back at Point One

Design always starts from a single point or pixel. That point or pixel is then repeated to make a line. In the repeated use of lines, their use and manner varies, creating shapes. A Triangular shape is formed from two diagonal lines and one horizontal line. There are also curves, which can be used to form circles. Each of these elements can come in different colors, sizes, weights and gestures that, when pieced together, create a composition. Design is visual.

As we understand how a graphic is made and how each element can affect perceptions, we learn to be fluent with it. In learning a new language, we start with letters and slowly build our vocabulary with words. We will do the same here as we dissect each element of visual design and learn how each element can be used to impact the design we intend to create.

Elements of Design

- **Line** is the most basic element in a design. It can divide, direct, conform, dissect and connect with other elements of design. Mostly, lines are used to create a connection between two or more elements in a design. A line can be portrayed in different strokes, weights and directions, and each of these variations can be vital in providing a character or emotion to the design.

- **Color** is the most obvious element in design. Most people recognize an artwork or design through its use of colors. Color can be used as a background, as a stand-alone, or with other elements. It is vital in creating a specific mood within a design. Creating color that harmonizes with itself and with other elements of a design is also important. Each color has its own unique meaning, and one attribute of a good designer is a strong grasp of color.

- **Shape** is where things form slowly. Shapes are defined by boundaries of lines and colors, and they are often used to create a focal point or a specific subject matter. The use of shapes is vital in a good design, as shapes can be the base of each design. However, shapes can be overused.

- **Space** is an area where elements are placed or an area devoid of elements. Space is often overlooked by designers, as they tend to focus on lines and shapes, but it is just as vital as the other elements.

- **Texture** is a quality that allows an element to have a three-dimensional look. Every element is subject to texture, and a bad use of texture can definitely destroy the intended use of the design.

- **Typography** is the use of letters and words within a design. Good typography helps convey the message in the simplest form, using as few words as possible. Bad typography draws the audience's attention away from the design. Typography especially crucial in web designs and in print designs.

- **Scale** refers to the varying dimensions/sizes of each element within a design. Playing with scale allows the designer to connect elements to one another and to hold them toward a common standard.

Each designer's goal should be to handle these elements wisely, and a strong understanding of each element is needed to orchestrate a quality design.

Line

A designer should be able to discern the different qualities of lines, and especially their purposes in a design. A line can be helpful in directing movement, dissecting sections, differentiating elements and connecting pieces. It is up to the designer to decide how to wisely use these meanings. Lines can even be implied. If 3 to 5 elements are aligned horizontally, your mind will fill in the gaps with a line.

Lines can serve as divider; this is often seen in magazine layouts. Lines are also used within grids, wherein a framework of intersecting lines provides a handy guide to use when placing elements within a composition. Lines are used to explain the "rule of thirds." This is a rule of thumb for artists that guides the placement of a design's focal point. According to the rule of thirds, focal points should be placed at the intersections of two equally spaced horizontal lines and two equally spaced vertical lines. If the focal point is placed in this way, the composition benefits from more interest, tension and energy than when the focal point is simply placed in the center of the composition.

Lines can also serve as the edges of shapes. These lines close out shapes' boundaries in a tangible and visual way. A line directs your mind to look at shapes more directly and easily.

Lines can also add meaning to an image. In some cartoons, for instance, a pattern of horizontal lines serves as an indicator that the subject is moving. A wavy line above a character can indicate dizziness, and vertical lines above a subject can portray the subject as falling. Lines are often used in portraying movement.

Lines are also used in organizing the placement of elements, especially in web designs and print layouts. Aligning objects with a common baseline helps to neatly present content. Having a margin set off with a line helps keep the audience's attention where it should be.

Each of these uses should direct the audience's attention and convey a specific attribute or characteristic.

Color

Colors can be used to convey emotion without being too obvious. Every color chosen affects a composition both visually and contextually. While a designer should always feel free to choose colors for aesthetic reasons, a careful approach to choosing colors helps reinforce a design. An understanding of color psychology is needed for this. Keep in mind that a color's can vary in different cultures and that the designer is responsible for owning the colors he/she intends to use and directing these colors to a specific emotion. Some general meanings of colors include:

- red = anger, heat

- blue = corporations, coolness

- purple = royalty, sophistication

- yellow = warmth, cowardice

- black = death, elegance

- green = nature, health

In learning how to design, you should be able to discern inappropriate color schemes, such as a red background for a corporate design. The meanings of colors help explain why most fast-food chains have red in their logos and most corporate businesses incorporate blue in their logos.

Designers should also consider color harmony. The color wheel can be helpful in choosing colors for a design. By using it, we can devise different harmonious color pairings that should work well in graphic designs.

Some color themes are the following:

- Analogous colors are any three colors that are side-by-side on a 12-part color wheel, such as yellow, yellow-orange and orange. Usually, one of the three colors cuts through the others.

- Complementary colors are any two colors that are directly opposite each other on a color wheel, such as red and green or red-purple and yellow-green.

Beyond the color itself, its relationship with other colors should also be a factor in design. Analyzing the effects colors have on one another provides a good head start in understanding the relativity of color. The relationship between the values, saturations and warmth/coolness of respective hues can cause noticeable differences in our perceptions of color. The designer should feel comfortable choosing the color palette that best complements his design, which is only accomplished through practice.

Observe other designs' use of colors and analyze how they benefited the design.

Shapes

Shapes are two-dimensional areas with discernable outlines. They can be open or closed, angular or round, and big or small.

Shapes can be used in designing graphics to organize information, symbolize ideas, emphasize specific content, and create a sense of movement, depth or texture. Designers often use shapes to sustain interest in a design.

There are a number of ways shapes can be used, and like lines, they are an essential building block in a designer's visual vocabulary. It is important to understand the different uses of shapes and to learn to appropriately use them within a design.

Space

An important reminder to all designers about the use of space within a design is that a blank area is as important as a filled area. Positive space refers to the areas that are filled with elements, and negative space refers to the areas that are deliberately left blank to imply content. Many designers tend to fill every space like they would do on a fill-in-the-blank quiz. Creating a good composition with harmony among its elements, however, requires an insightful consideration of negative space.

The use of space must serve a purpose in communication instead of just being the channel for the various techniques that a designer uses. A small element that is placed in a small space seems insignificant compared to an element that occupies more space.

Texture

Texture is a decorative element within a design. It adds character to an element, but keep in mind that it can also be overused. It can add visual detail to a shape or even to typography, helping to portray the subject in a realistic and emotional manner.

Keeping in mind the power of texture in design, we must be intentional in its use. Just because we can always add textures doesn't necessarily mean that we *should* always add them. Texture can be distracting, and so some designers minimize their use of textures. However, some designers know how to add textures in a manner that they become a part of the focus instead of distracting from it.

You are free to find and develop your own style in using textures. Experiment with various styles and textures and practice with them long enough to build confidence in your use of textures.

Typography

Typography is crucial in delivering a message in the simplest fashion. Good typography strongly reinforces the design, and bad typography distracts from the intended message. Typography is more than just the font choice. There are a lot of factors a designer can play with to deliver fine typography, including scale, contrast, kerning, legibility and weight. The goal of typography is to get a message across.

Readability must come first. The designer should choose a font that is easy to read before thinking about its aesthetics. Readability is usually based on a clean look, especially for websites or print publications that have articles or a lot of text.

Different font styles have corresponding feels. Some add a modern feel to the design, and others add a rather casual look. It is important to get a grasp of each font's feel. A designer must also be familiar with how a font is commonly used. Observe various print ads from different fields and observe how each font matches with the aesthetic of the design. Serif fonts (which have tails at each end of a stroke, as seen in Times New Roman or Gentium) are often used in elegant designs. Sans-serif fonts (which lack these tails, as in Helvetica) are used in modern designs. Script fonts can be used to add a playful look to the design. Each of these styles should be used creatively and appropriately.

Learning how to pair fonts help a designer deliver good typography. Serif fonts match well with sans-serif fonts; often, two serif fonts or two sans-serif fonts will clash visually because they are too similar. The key is to add a considerable contrast between fonts while maintaining a complementary look. Avoid clashing moods in paired fonts. Consider the content hierarchy as you choose fonts, and highlight this hierarchy through the use of color and scale. Normally, two fonts work well in a design, but using more than two fonts can be risky. The key to choosing a font is to keep it simple and clean.

Keep the kerning (the spaces in between the letters) consistent throughout each word. Some fonts may have bad kerning between letters by default, so be cautious when using them.

Scale

Scale can be an effective tool in highlighting one element or keeping a balance throughout a design. By careful consideration, the designer can use scale to reflect the intended hierarchy of the elements. Keep the scale balanced throughout by understanding the spaces between the elements. Every space within a design has a function, whether the designer notices that function or not. It is up to the designer to be intentional with each element's scale. Scale helps define harmony and balance throughout the design, so the designer must grasp this concept to make the design look right.

To use these elements effectively, we have what is commonly known among designers as the design principles. These principles are the skeletal foundation on which all techniques of design should stand. Without these principles, even with the finest techniques, a design may fall flat. Understanding how the principles work can guide us in creating an effective design.

Here is a brief definition of each principle:

Principles of Design

- **Balance** is the distribution of the visual weight in a design. A design can be intentionally symmetrical or asymmetrical, but in a good design, the designer properly considers the elements' balance. The designer must check the balance of the composition to maintain the intended aesthetic.

- **Repetition** is the intentional use of the same elements to create a sense of rhythm and order within a design. Repetition helps establish an association among various elements. Some designers use repetition to establish a rhythm and then disrupt it with a contrasting element to create a strong, dynamic design. A repeated use of dissimilar elements is called a pattern.

- **Contrast** is the juxtaposition of dissimilar elements to create interest or tension. A specific element can be highlighted by the use of contrast. Usually, a designer uses this to lead the viewer's attention to an intended subject, but contrast also is used to add depth to a design.

- **Proximity** is a lack of space between elements that creates a relationship and introduces a hierarchy of information.

Proper use of proximity each element to take an appropriate amount of space within the design.

- **Composition** is the analytic placement of elements on a background through the use of scale and proximity. A well-composed design leads the viewer toward a focal point.

- **Harmony** is the peaceful relationship of elements used in a design. Harmony holds the pieces of a design together through the use of complementary colors, rhythm, and proximity.

- **Alignment** is the arrangement of elements on a grid beneath the design. Well-aligned elements help organize the design, especially in designs that have a lot of written content.

Observe other works, and see for yourself how each principle can manifest and how each principle helps to convey a design's message. Your critical analysis of each of those designs will build your personal design convictions.

As graphic designers, we must practice these principles diligently, but as creative people, we must also learn how to choose our style using these principles. Practices and styles differ from one designer to another, but the key is to be brave enough to hone a style of your own. We can follow many trends, and we can use these trends as guides, but it is still, ultimately, your choice on how these principles should interact with one another.

Chapter Two: Who Graphic Designers Are

Due to today's rising need for clean visual aesthetics and the relentless pace of technology, graphic designers more than ever need to learn to design efficiently. This job does more than make the world colorful and fancy; rather, it provides solutions to objectives through the use of visual language. A successful graphic designer needs a fluent, clear, and concise visual language.

To become an effective graphic designer, one must understand how the design process should help. Most graphic designers approach each design methodically by understanding the problem that needs to be solved, creating some sample designs, deciding what works and what does not work, and then coming up with a solution. We can apply this process ourselves. In our efforts to understand what works and what does not work, it is important to first understand the purpose of the design before creating any sample designs. We then can examine selected works that can influence our design.

As we collect ideas and inspirations prior to designing, we let what we collected bleed through to our design. Our inspirations seep into the canvas, and we design accordingly with the provided design brief. Other designers don't depend too much on finding inspirations, as they have a strong set of design convictions that have served them well. It is all a matter of choice, after all, and whatever works for each designer should be the goal.

A successful graphic designer knows to create a visual, regularly curates his/her portfolio, publishes works and enjoys his/her craft.

In this chapter, we go through different identities that a successful graphic designer can project.

Visual Problem-Solvers

In addition to learning how to produce visual aesthetics, a designer should know how to communicate – both inside and outside of a design. Whether through a spoken or a written pitch, you should know how to intrigue those you share your design briefs with. Creating a strong impression helps others perceive your value in presenting ideas, making you seem indispensable. When others see your strong grasp of your craft, your designs are more likely to be well-received.

Get into the habit of looking through a situation with a solution in mind; designers are problem-solvers. Come into this job with the mindset that your designs should create a positive impact. The work you do should be not just pretty but functional and accessible. Your designs should represent the intended ideals, not your personal creative expression. That's what makes communication vital. As a graphic designer, you learn how to collaborate with people around you, and you have to keep in mind, for instance, that not everyone around you knows the Photoshop jargon that you know.

Sometimes, a client will ask you to create a design, and it is the job of the graphic designer to find out what the client wants. Instead of painstakingly designing countless revisions for a clueless client, learn the design's objective. This immensely helps the designer to know what the client wants and how the design should look.

Understanding the design brief and its objectives is just as important as executing the design itself. Taking the time to chat about a project with your client will definitely help minimize revisions. In doing this, you also help keep the workflow pleasant and conducive for creativity.

Modern-Day Artisans

In the medieval era, artisans were known to be highly individualized in their work. They were often classified by the craft that they specialized in. They were masters of that specific craft. They developed a love of their craft and devoted their entire lives to it, and oftentimes, they earned their reputation from their work. They prided themselves on the quality of their work and showed dedication and passion for each product that they worked on. There was always a personal connection between the artisan and the client.

It was only in the first half of the 19th century that the tradition of artisans was disrupted by corporations beginning to industrialize. The demand for faster workflows resulted in greater efficiency, but this type of efficiency compromised the individuality of each product. It made the relationship between clients and artisans impersonal. Then, to commercialize products so that they could be mass-produced, the artisans had to choose to either focus on their craft or to be paid more to work in factories. Suddenly, words like "employer" and "employee" emerged to replace "artisan" and "client."

As graphic designers, it is our goal to treat our craft with the same amount of passion an artisan would have. Like artisans, we should hone our craft, specialize in it, innovate with it and use it to earn a reputation. We have to love our craft deeply enough to practice it daily. We need to take pride in our work and hold ourselves accountable; only then will others notice our specialty.

The field of graphic design includes an expansive list of resources and styles. We have access to many tutorials and design inspirations that we can pattern our works after. This can be an advantage or a disadvantage. It is an advantage for a learner who understands a new concept well enough to develop it further into his own style, but it is a disadvantage for a learner who uses it as a template for all future work. A successful designer knows how to work toward a personal style rather than creating carbon copies of other designers' work. To stand out among designers who have learned from the same sources, we must develop our own voices.

The field is expanding; it now spans web design, logo design, typography, print design, UI (user interface) design and UX (user experience) design. A graphic designer knows how to navigate each of these fields, and with the expansive resources available, this is doable. A versatile designer learns a bit from each of these fields and develops a portfolio in each field. As you progress toward each classification, your personal preferences should translate into your work so that your personal style becomes evident in each work. Learn to commodify your work in ways that do not compromise your personal standards. Develop work in each field while being conscious of your works. If a task does not interest you, hold yourself accountable as you remember your personal accountability for the quality of work that you produce. Stake your reputation on each work, and be bold.

Anyone Can Be a Graphic Designer

You don't need to be great at drawing. You don't need to be a born into a family of artists or know how to render art realistically. You don't have to be innovative. You do have to enjoy the craft, however, and be able to add personality to your designs. You don't need to own the latest technology, but you do need to have critical thinking skills to understand what each design element adds and takes away. You need to think visually.

We have to eliminate the misconceptions that a graphic designer is born or that a person must have been drawing since an early age to succeed in the field. Through the advent of Adobe Photoshop and other software, anyone can have the digital resources to produce visual designs. Anyone can learn graphic design, and anyone can approach this field with a curious mindset.

Critical thinking is the most important skill to should work on if you'd like to be a graphic designer. Learning the tools and software will also help you start a career in graphic design. Learn the basics of Photoshop. If you're into sketching and logo designs, become familiar with Adobe Illustrator, too. If you're into web design, learn the basics of Adobe Muse. All this software should help you to establish your principles as a graphic designer. Look through the designs that you encounter in your daily routine and use them to practice your critical thinking. What is the message of each design? How does the design help convey a message? Ponder these questions. The knowledge you attain through daily practice is still key to your success. A lot of graphic designers bank on their previous experience to land a job, and they lose their edge and their hunger to learn. Thus, they become stagnant in their designs. Learn to be actively curious. Don't wait for inspiration to strike – everything is interesting if you look deeply enough. This might be the edge that you could have over countless other graphic designers.

Feed your creativity with passions outside of design. Some of the most successful designers have another creative outlet that helps feed their designs. Some learn analog photography, some like to bike around town, some hike, and some read novels. All these hobbies can help diversify your skill as a graphic designer and can be incorporated into your designs.

Finally, look around your world. Keep your eyes focused on what interests you – often, these sights can be added to your design, where they will also captivate your audience.

In short, if you want to be a graphic designer, learn by doing.

Chapter Three: How Graphic Design Works

Graphic design fills a role in every field. Lawyers, dentists, hospitals, and athletes all need websites and logos. With the rise of the social media, the need for design has grown even more. With the large number of choices a graphic designer can face, taking up a specialization within the field will help you focus.

A Career as a Corporate Graphic Designer

First and foremost, look at your résumé and personal branding. This is your first task as a graphic designer, even before you take your first professional contract. This package includes your educational background, skillset, work ethic and personality in a visual aesthetic that reflects you. Discover your tendencies as a designer, work toward them, and show them in your personal branding. This project provides you with freedom that serves yourself. Know what works for you and what doesn't. Be insightful in creating these visuals.

However, don't lose control of this kind of freedom, as you might overdo it. Having a creative résumé filled with the latest trends in design might not get you the job that you want. A résumé still has the purpose of communicating. It has to be legible and not distracting. Simplicity is a good aim, but presenting yourself in a simple aesthetic can be quite complex, so you have to be insightful.

Keep your résumé organized and concise. Approach your personal résumé as you would approach any other design process – consider the context, the objectives and the audience. Overloading your résumé with art will distract those who could hire you. Be concise, removing whatever is not needed and keeping the design as clean as possible. Remember that your résumé will be stacked with other résumés. Attend to the details of your résumé, as it has to be pixel-perfect.

Include a curated portfolio in your application. Always place your best work first. Your best work should be close to your heart; it may not have been paid work. This should add value to your résumé, as it shows that you are willing to initiate projects for the sake of your craft. Develop your passion for the craft by first honing a specialty and then, as you expand your tastes, translating your specialized preference to those expanded tastes. Also be sure to show work that relate to the real world and to communicate how you approached this work.

As you work for a company, always try to increase your value within the company. As a visual problem-solver, understand each design brief they present to you, and be ready to take initiative to deliver the necessary design. Be ready for criticisms; welcome them as tools for improvement. This is when effective communication is necessary. Within a company, you're going to collaborate with businessmen, architects, engineers, marketing strategists and salespeople. Each will; see your work differently. As a designer, you should welcome their specialized perspectives, as they always add depth and functionality to your work.

Build your reputation with your work like an artisan would. Be approachable yet firm, and learn how to prioritize. Cultivate good relationships, as how others see you affects how they see your designs. Cultivate a pleasant working environment to enhance creativity. Make yourself known to others in the company to help your chances for a promotion. Be transparent with your workflows and designs, and allow feedback to pass through your thought process as you design.

Don't get lost within the corporate ladder. Have a personal career map. With this, you will learn how to prioritize and how to remove clutter from your workflow. Consider the lifestyle that you want to incorporate in your life, and have this goal in mind.

A Career as a Freelance Graphic Designer

You have to value your work highly if you're aiming to be a freelance graphic designer. The value of your designs should be credible. You should add value to your work by polishing, developing and organizing it. As a freelance designer, you are held accountable for every step in your workflow; these steps may add clutter to your lifestyle, and so, to have a successful career as a freelance graphic designer, organization is a must.

You have to streamline your workflow. You own your time as a freelance graphic designer, but don't let that fool you into thinking that you have the freedom to procrastinate. You will be bombarded with deadlines. Stay focused on your projects, as creative people have the tendency to have many "in-progress" projects. To be a successful graphic designer, aim to finish the project efficiently and within the deadline; even better, finish it beforehand.

Learning keyboard shortcuts in your chosen software is a must. Save old work and use it as templates for future projects. Learn to schedule your time if you work from home. Consistency can add to your organization. Having a set schedule for freelance work and for rest should reduce the stress that can accumulate as you pile up projects.

As a freelance graphic designer, you have to build a solid network. Connect with other designers to expand your circle; these connections can also influence your work positively. The lifestyle of a freelance graphic designer is quite interesting, as you own your time and work from home, but that lifestyle can become a rut if there's no social network to attend to. Develop a portfolio and have a personal website. A practical tip is to have your portfolio hosted on site other than your website, as this can save you time on website revisions and portfolio management. Develop personal branding and create a social presence. Just like in the corporate setting, you have to let your presence be felt, especially as you try to attract clients. Create a solid identity through social media, and ensure that the information you put out is reliable. Have an interesting account − writing design-related articles and blogging about your experiences can help you stand out from other freelancers. Collect your personal projects and publish them online

As a freelance designer, learning to take care of yourself is a must. Don't take on too many projects at once, and learn to say no to projects that you would not excel on. Protect yourself from frugal clients by having contracts. Don't ever work without a firm contract. The contract protects both sides, so it must be treated with care. Be vigilant in guarding all your works as you post them online. Copyright your works. You have these rights as soon as you have produced the work, although in some cases, clients will own the copyright for your works, so be sure to talk with these clients before displaying the works online. Learn to market yourself appropriately. As you learn to value your skills and experience as a graphic designer, you should never undermine these by cutting your fees. Take pride in the work that you do, and price yourself appropriately. Your fees reflect your skills as a designer.

Conclusion

The design industry is vast, and specializing in a field should boost your credibility. You should choose wisely and devote your time to this field. Love it like a craft that your reputation can be staked upon. Ironically, the design world is still small. What this means is that the networks you create within the design industry can take you places and connect you to people. Thus, you should build a healthy reputation, always be nice and cooperative when working with other professionals, and have a positive outlook. This career is enjoyable; once you learn to practice your creativity, the satisfaction you would get from seeing your work impact lives around you will be euphoric.

The life of a graphic designer is a very interesting one; as you meet people and get to understand their needs, you learn how you can help them with your visual creativity. Always remember the fundamentals, develop your core traits as a designer, specialize in a single field, and preserve a curious outlook toward other fields. Incorporate, collaborate, publish and copyright. You are providing – more than the skills and work ethic – the psychology of the design. Understand how you can help people and delight yourself with design. Learn all these skills, and you'll be on your way to becoming a successful graphic designer.

www.ingramcontent.com/pod-product-compliance
Lightning Source LLC
Chambersburg PA
CBHW060353290526
45791CB00004B/1652